I've been following Shauna's blog and slurping it up every time. Her relevant, practical, and effective wisdom jumps up like a fairy godmother and gives you new perspective. Like when you put that one, perfect dash of red lipstick on... it sits right with me, with my motherhood, with my calling and role as a wife and mom and friend. Making a LIFE CHANGING impact on my identity and how I wear it everyday.

I am so excited about her book! It will most definitely have a place next to my bedside, and not just on the bookshelf!

Roné

What a blessing! Shauna has done so well capturing the thoughts of a mom in her many seasons. Life comes at different times and this book will be effective no matter what chapter you are reading. Very rich and honest—not a book to just read through quickly. It will bring loads of open discussions and intimate prayer times as you soak in the words. I so enjoyed reading this, and I'm sure that it will bless and encourage so many people.

Laura

There is no doubt that you will be empowered and equipped by the wisdom poured out so gracefully and authentically throughout this book. Shauna has impacted my life in ways that can now be measured as I have applied her wisdom and insight as a mom of two boys (ages two and five). I cheer you on!

Menaka

Twenty-five years ago I was a new mommy looking for my lost identity between never-ending diapers, an overstretched budget, and sleep deprivation. Shauna's book would have made life so much easier for me! She presents the attributes of the woman in Proverbs 31, not as an unattainable standard, but as our identity. These attributes become ours as we yield to the Father's Spirit of grace.

This book is a must-read for mothers in the thick of kids' chaos... and not-yet-moms... and moms, like me, who have an empty nest and are asking, *"What kind of mom have I been? Who am I now that my kids have left home?"*

Marian

This book was challenging... and I want to read it again! I was so inspired to keep going, and the best part was that Shauna was so REAL. I loved the "Let's Chat" parts and the prayers, and all of those verses in the back for us to memorize. I'm definitely going to do that.

Vanessa

I highly recommend this book if you need encouragement as a busy mom. Shauna's refreshing take on motherhood and Godly wisdom will lift your spirits and always direct you straight back to Jesus. She is always ready with a relatable story that brings life and hope, and her book is no different.

Christy

IDENTITY

Finding the Proverbs 31 Woman in the Middle of Kid Chaos

For every woman experiencing Identity Crisis and asking herself, *"Who am I really?"*

By Shauna Blaak

Published by Blaaklist Writers

She laughs
without fear
of the future

ISBN: 978-0-620-74230-6 (print)
ISBN: 978-0-620-75749-2 (e-book)

Author: Shauna Blaak
Cover Design: Lise-Mari Coetzee, Coetzee Publishing
Cover Image: Impact Photography and Design Studio
Published by: Blaaklist Writers Publishing

Dedication

This book is dedicated to all of the beautiful mommies that I've been privileged to walk with over the years. *(You know who you are.)*

Thank you, dear friends, for going on this lovely journey with me. Oh, how you've blessed me with the generous way you've welcomed me into your lives. No, we may not be biological family, we may not even be citizens of the same country, but what an incredible privilege to become lifelong friends. You've made MY life richer for having invited me into yours.

My deepest prayer for you is that you know, deep down in your spirit, that

---

YOU ARE LOVED and YOU CAN DO THIS

Table of Contents

Special Thanks

This book would not have been possible without the tireless support of my amazing family and friends.

To my darling, Erwin, who has never competed with me for 'first place.' You are my most faithful fan and my greatest hero! Thanks for loving me and encouraging me, and for reminding me all the time that, *"The Source of all creativity lives inside of me, and His name is Jesus! I will never run out of things to write!"* I'll love you forever, honey!

To Raelynne who always makes me feel like the prettiest and the smartest mom around. I love sending you my work because I know you'll always be encouraging and honest. You are so good at what you do, and you give your momma so much joy!

To Joshua who fearlessly rebukes me with a *"Shut yo' pie-hole, Woman"* whenever I start giving in to fear and insecurity. (No, he's not disrespectful. That's his light-hearted way of saying, *"No more fear, Mom. You can do this!"*) Thanks, Josh, I hear ya!

To David who is proving to be an excellent proofreader and collaborator. Thank you for always being willing to check out your mom's work, rub her tense shoulders, and for always having an educated opinion on style. I'm so blessed to have you in my life!

To Rachel who is the perfect example of passion and zest for life. You never seem to tire of honing your talent and learning new things. *I want to be like you when I grow up, Baby Girl. Keep going!*

To Lise-Mari and Charl who were the catalysts to me thinking bigger and brighter. I would've never started without your confidence and encouragement. You believed in me long before I ever believed in myself, and you empowered me to start this incredible journey. Thank you!

To the many talented photographers and designers who have blessed me with their incredible talents:

- Lise-Mari Coetzee, Coetzee Publishing
- Impact Photography and Design Studio
- Catherine Swayde Photography & Design
- Asher Love Photography
- Martesia Bezuidenhout Photography
- Nicole Honeywell
- Raelynne Blaak

This book is so beautiful because you guys are so amazing!

To those wonderfully picky women in my life who edited and proofread the manuscript: Marian, Almari, Laura, Menaka, Vanessa, Christy, Laetitia, and my mom, Lydia. I am deeply grateful for your incredible wisdom, perfectionism, and OCD tendencies. Thank you for catching the things I could no longer see.

To Almari and Jandré for being the answer to my desperate prayer for "help" when it came to marketing this book. Thank you for believing in me and pushing me out of my comfort zone. You guys are brilliant, and I am so grateful!

And last but not least... thank You, Father God, for having better plans for my life than I ever dreamed possible. You give me confidence when I am weak. You give me wisdom when I am confused. You give me family when I am lonely. You give me security when I am lost. You've given me everything I need for life and godliness, and I am so grateful to be Your girl. Thank You, Father, for the privilege of writing this book. I love You so much!

Introduction

Every mom faces that moment when she looks in the mirror and asks herself, *"Oh my gosh! Who is that person?"*

If that's you, I'm here to assure you that you are completely NORMAL. You aren't crazy, insane, or losing your mind (yes, I know those are synonyms... I was trying to get your attention).

I can explain what's happening to you in two words: IDENTITY CRISIS.

The journey of Motherhood is a series of Defining and Re-Defining moments.

And with every change of season, you need to bravely ask yourself this question, *"Who am I now?"*

IDENTITY CRISIS #1 - Babies

Surprise! The world that you knew and loved has suddenly and irreversibly changed forever. You are now living on another planet. Who the heck are these short people around me, and why are they so noisy? And you ask yourself,

• Who am I when I no longer have a career, paycheck, or peers who make me feel good about myself?

• Who am I when I no longer have intelligent conversations with adults?

• Who am I when all I do is take care of babies all... day... long?"

IDENTITY CRISIS #2 – School Years

You've just left your baby in the care of an overly 'smiley' Kindergarten teacher who entices them with snacks and toys, and you can't stop your tears.

"I'm happy. Really, I am."

You suddenly have a few hours to spend without children underfoot... but you have no idea what to do with yourself. So, you cry into your Starbucks and ask,

• *Who am I when I have time to myself but don't know what I like to do anymore?*

• *What should I do with my time and energy?*

• *How do I bring value and purpose to my life apart from caring for babies?*

And then comes **IDENTITY CRISIS #3 – Empty Nest**

Welcome to my world. Our oldest two kids are out of the house and studying internationally, one in Australia, and the other in Canada. The other two are in high school here in South Africa, but they don't need as much hands-on help as they used to.

And I look in the mirror, refusing to let the tears ruin my mascara *again*, and ask,

• *Who am I when the kids don't need me anymore?*

• *What do I want to do with the rest of my life? (Which could also read, 'Who do I want to be when I grow up?')*

• *Do I even remember the dreams I used to have? Or do I have new dreams now? How do I fill the hours in my day to reach those dreams?*

IDENTITY CRISIS #4 - Grandchildren

Or perhaps you are well into other stages of identity crisis such as being Grandparents, and you're asking,

• *Who am I when I know all the answers, but they don't want to listen?*

• *Who am I when the world is changing faster than I can program my DVD player?*

• *Who am I when the grandkids are miles away and they don't even know me?*

IDENTITY CRISIS #5 – Trauma

Or perhaps, Heaven forbid, you are finding yourself in horrible circumstances that are completely out of your control. Death, divorce, disease, and disaster all have a way of rocking our world to the core, and causing us to ask,

• Who am I when my world has just collapsed and I can't even breathe?

You may be thinking, *"Seriously? Am I going to go through Identity Crisis more than once? I can't take it anymore."*

Well, my friend, brace yourself. This is going to be a long and wild ride.

Discovering and Rediscovering your Identity is a Life-Long Adventure

It doesn't happen just once. These are questions we must answer with each changing season.

And each time you are faced with change, you have a choice to make:

1. Do you want to stay stuck where you are, looking backward at the past, and letting depression steal your joy for today?

2. Or are you willing to REDEFINE yourself and allow God to fill you with fresh IDENTITY—happy, purposeful, and ready for the next season of your life?

When Identity Crisis hit me last year, I refused to get depressed and sing *'down-down-doobie-doo-down.'* It was time to look in the mirror and be honest,

"Shauna, WHO do you want to be NOW?"

I felt God challenging me to RE-INVENT myself. So, here's what I did:

1. I started my writing business—Blaaklist Writers

I've dreamed about it for years, but thanks to some dear friends who 'lit a fire under my butt,' I finally did it. I am now freelancing on Upwork.com and doing so well.

2. I started my blog—blaaklistwriters.com

It began as a 'passion project' to help me find my voice. The fun part was tapping into those deep wells of experience and wisdom that lay dormant inside me. What a fantastic journey!

3. I wrote this book… Finally!

This book is also a 'passion project' for me—the next step in my journey of IDENTITY. I've had the privilege of walking with some fabulous women over the years (young, old, and in-between), and they've been asking me for years to write a book.

I feel Father saying that 'Now is the Time' to share my life, my stories, and His love with these beautiful mommies.

And everyone said, *"It's about time!"*

How to Use This Book

Here's what you'll find in every chapter:

1. A story or poem to inspire you!

Many of these stories first appeared on my Blog (blaaklistwriters.com) and may sound familiar. I have especially included the posts that you loved the first time around.

2. LET'S CHAT... ♥ Questions for Discussion

I know how busy you are—I also had four kids under the age of six.

So, take a deep breath and relax. Look for the ♥s. These are questions to discuss with your friends over coffee. Let them stir up conversations and discover for yourself that collaboration is an awesome thing.

You were never meant to walk this road alone anyway!

3. LET'S PRAY...

I realize that sometimes you are just too tired to formulate thoughts and words. That's ok. These prayers are here to help you. You can pray them for yourself, or you can change them up.

But do pray something—PRAYER IS POWERFUL.

4. NOTES...

If you are a sleep-deprived mom and you find your keys in the fridge regularly, this section is for you.

When God shows you something important about your identity (and He will), do yourself a favour and WRITE IT DOWN.

We ALL need to remember Words of Life from our Father.

So, grab yourself a coffee and enjoy!

1. You Were Never Meant to Walk this Road Alone

My arrival was met with bloodshot eyes and abject failure. Baby was finally asleep, but mommy was 'finished.'

Day 3... Why does no one warn you about day 3?

"How are you, my friend?"

The tears started afresh and out of her mouth gushed all of the insecurity and self-doubt that had ravaged her heart and mind for the last hours.

"I can't do this. I'm failing. What is wrong with him? What is wrong with me? I'm so tired. I'm so sore. I can't even think straight. Why am I crying? Why is he still crying? Oh, my God, I think I'm gonna die."

I hugged her and let her spend her tears on my shoulder. I remember that truck, the one that rolls over you without warning, over and over and over again. Her real mother was an ocean away, and I felt the weight of maternal compassion. When the tears were spent, she sat, and I made her tea.

"What am I going to do?" she asked me.

I gently looked in her eyes, and answered, *"Well, the first thing you are gonna do is open that door there."* (On the other side of their apartment door lived thirty-five gap-year students who were aching to hug their friend and see her beautiful baby).

"Noooo, I can't. Look at me! I'm a mess. I don't want them to see me like this. I don't even know what I'm doing yet."

"I know," I said gently, *"but YOU WERE NEVER MEANT TO WALK THIS ROAD ALONE."*

"The Word says that 'God sets the lonely in families…' (Psalm 68:6). We are your family, my darling friend. You are no longer alone.

"The very reason that today feels so horrible is that there is no one here to share it with you. Those people outside that door, they are the answer to your pain. You are empty, and they have love to spend on you. You need to let them in.

"Just open the door."

So we made a plan. I baked some brownies and brewed the coffee. She washed away her tears and then rested on the couch.

And when the time was right, we opened the door together.

Thirty-five walked in, not including the multitude who floated in unawares. We saw and felt the difference. Eager young people lavished hugs and compliments to both mom and baby, and ministering angels brought comfort, encouragement, confidence, hope, peace... and the first glimmers of joy again.

Oh miraculous wonder, that God uses His children to be HIS hands and HIS voice.

And the atmosphere changed.

LET'S CHAT...

This true account of my dear friend is far too common, isn't it? Not just among first-time mommies, but people in general. We shouldn't be surprised—one of the enemy's oldest tricks is to 'divide and conquer.'

♥ Can you recall a time when you felt completely overwhelmed and alone? What happened? What did you do?

♥ Why do you think women (and men) isolate themselves like that?

♥ What does the Bible say about it? (Read Proverbs 18:1)

♥ When was the last time you noticed someone (whether friend or acquaintance) 'disappear' without warning?

♥ Can you think of someone right now who could use some encouragement and a call from you?

We were never meant to walk alone.

LET'S PRAY...

Father, thank You for the many ways that you take care of me. I am so grateful that You don't expect me to do this on my own. Thank You for "placing me in a family" where I can laugh and cry, learn and grow, and let down the walls around my heart.

Father, I'm so sorry for all of the times that my pride and fear keep me from reaching out for help. I repent for being too proud to open the door and let people into my life. Please help me to realize that I don't have to be perfect and that "it's ok."

I also ask that You would open my eyes to see other women who have disappeared for no reason. Help me to be attentive to the needs around me, and to express Your hands and heart toward them. Help me to be courageous enough to "Go, *find them, and call them back from the isolation.*"

I love you, Jesus! Amen.

NOTES...

NOTES...

2. You ARE a Proverbs 31 Woman

The Proverbs 31 Woman—you either love her, or you hate her. She will either inspire you to greatness, or she will remind you of your weakness.

Rising early, working late? No thanks. I can't compete with that. I am definitely not a morning person. Does that really mean that I'm NOT a Proverbs 31 woman too?

Great. More guilt!

Years ago, when the kids were little, I remember having a conversation with the Father in the middle of Walmart, of all places. *(Yes, God shops at Walmart.)*

I had been complaining to Him about how busy I was. I couldn't compete with all of the other SuperMoms around me who 'really had it together.' I wasn't rich enough. I wasn't smart enough. I wasn't skinny enough. I wasn't popular enough.

> I remember saying, *"Sheesh, God. Proverbs 31 sucks. It's not fair that I have to do ALL of this stuff and Erwin doesn't. He just gets to be the husband and be served all the time. I'm so tired. I can't keep doing this."*

In hindsight, I realize now that Erwin had never demanded these things of me. It was I who put unrealistic expectations on myself, trying desperately to be the 'good wife.' I was trying to live up to the Proverbs 31 Woman and exhausting myself in the process. No wonder I didn't like her.

Out-of-the-blue, I had one of those almost-audible moments of hearing God's voice. This is what He said,

> **"Shauna, you are ALREADY a Proverbs 31 Woman. You see those boots in your cart?"**

(I had about six pairs of winter boots in my shopping cart. Walmart was having an incredible end-of-the-season sale, so I was buying every size available because I knew that at least one of my four kids would need them next year.)

> **"Well, that's just like verse 15, 'She rises early and provides for the needs of her household.' It's not about being a morning person and working yourself to death—it's about foreseeing the needs of your family BEFORE THEY ARE EVEN AWARE OF THEIR NEED.**

> **"Your kids don't even know they need boots next winter, but you do. You ARE a Proverbs 31 Woman!**

"I'm proud of you!"

That moment RADICALLY changed my perspective on Proverbs 31 and my abilities as a wife and mother.

I realized that I had been looking at this all wrong. It's not about working harder and performing better. Proverbs 31 isn't a crazy 'To Do List' that I have to get done in one day. No!

Proverbs 31 is a BLANK CHEQUE of purpose and destiny that I GET to accomplish in my lifetime!

What, seriously?

- I GET to buy and sell land.
- I GET to be creative and profitable.
- I GET to be strong and beautiful.

That's awesome! I'll take it!

LET'S CHAT...

Let's be honest here, COMPARISON is the silent killer of most women, isn't it? Comparing ourselves with the SuperMom down the street, or worse yet, the SuperMom on Facebook or some mommy blog. It's no wonder that many of us slip into silent depression and give up hope altogether.

But my friend, we don't need to live that way any longer. The enemy has been a master at speaking death to us for far too long. It is high time that we hear the Words of Life that our Father speaks over us.

♥ Read all of Proverbs 31:10-31 (NLT).

Before you roll your eyes and utter a *"Too busy—I'll pass,"* remember that this Scripture was written as a poem. It's figurative, not literal.

In fact, it was actually written in Hebrew as an acrostic poem (you know, the first line started with the Hebrew 'A,' the second started with 'B,' and so on). But it was also written in a sing-song fashion so that the young people of that day (both women and men) could easily memorize it. How cool is that?

Read it with fresh eyes. There are many hidden meanings within its word pictures.

A Wife of Noble Character

10 Who can find a virtuous and capable wife? She is more precious than rubies.

11 Her husband can trust her, and she will greatly enrich his life.

12 She brings him good, not harm, all the days of her life.

13 She finds wool and flax and busily spins it.

14 She is like a merchant's ship, bringing her food from afar.

15 She gets up before dawn to prepare breakfast for her household and plan the day's work for her servant girls.

16 She goes to inspect a field and buys it; with her earnings, she plants a vineyard.

17 She is energetic and strong, a hard worker.

18 She makes sure her dealings are profitable; her lamp burns late into the night.

19 Her hands are busy spinning thread, her fingers twisting fiber.

20 She extends a helping hand to the poor and opens her arms to the needy.

21 She has no fear of winter for her household, for everyone has warm clothes.

22 She makes her own bedspreads. She dresses in fine linen and purple gowns.

23 Her husband is well known at the city gates, where he sits with the other civic leaders.

24 She makes belted linen garments and sashes to sell to the merchants.

25 She is clothed with strength and dignity, and she laughs without fear of the future.

26 When she speaks, her words are wise, and she gives instructions with kindness.

27 She carefully watches everything in her household and suffers nothing from laziness.

28 Her children stand and bless her. Her husband praises her:

29 "There are many virtuous and capable women in the world, but you surpass them all!"

30 Charm is deceptive, and beauty does not last; but a woman who fears the Lord will be greatly praised.

31 Reward her for all she has done. Let her deeds publicly declare her praise.

♥ Now, take some time to go through this passage, verse by verse, and rewrite it in your own words. *MAKE IT YOUR OWN.* Use words like, "I GET to…"

For example, verse 11, *"Her husband can trust her, and she will greatly enrich his life,"* can read,

> *I GET to be a trustworthy person and bring incredible value to my husband, my family, and everyone I interact with. I am not a burden.*

Another example, verse 18, *"She makes sure her dealings are profitable; her lamp burns late into the night,"* can read,

> *I GET to be a powerful business woman and make a profit. I am not a victim, nor am I lazy. I can work late into the night, literally. But I can also work late into the night, figuratively, which means that I will have endurance LONG after others have quit. I am not a quitter.*

USE YOUR IMAGINATION, but don't get all religious about it. We are not re-writing Scripture here. We are simply <u>applying</u> it to our lives, in our own language, and in our own cultural context.

The Word says this in Ephesians 3:20-21 (NIV),

"Now to Him who is able to do immeasurably more than all we ask or IMAGINE, according to His power that is at work within us, to Him be glory in the church and in Christ Jesus throughout all generations, forever and ever! Amen."

God's plans for us are so much bigger and better than our imagination. But how can we believe for more, if we don't imagine anything?

My friends, exercise your imagination. Be creative. Be bold. Stir up faith to believe God for the BEST for your life.

DOES THIS SOUND TOO DIFFICULT?

No problem!

I've created a FREE **"Companion Guide to Finding the Proverbs 31 Woman"** which I send to all of the subscribers to my blog.

If you haven't received yours yet, head over to www.blaaklistwriters.com and subscribe now!

♥ Using post-it notes, write out some of these Words of Life and post them around the house where you most need to read them (i.e., on the bathroom mirror, beside your bed, on the fridge, in the nursery).

This is a powerful exercise in speaking Words of Life to yourself.

————————————♥————————————

LET'S PRAY...

Father, I can't keep comparing myself to other women around me. It's driving me crazy and making me miserable.

Please forgive me for avoiding Proverbs 31. Father, breathe life on this passage of Scripture. Help me to hear Your voice. Speak to my mind and my heart, and show me the amazing things You have planned for my life.

Please forgive me for choosing to believe the negative things that the enemy has been saying about me. He's a liar, and I don't have to listen to him anymore.

I choose to listen to Your Words of Life for me. I choose to believe Your heart for me.

I choose to embrace my future and destiny!

Thank You, Father.

Amen

————————————♥————————————

NOTES...

NOTES...

NOTES...

I am a Proverbs 31
woman
blaaklistwriters.com

The image on the back is designed specifically for you!

Cut it out, frame it, or simply post it wherever you need to be inspired.

3. Girl, You'd Better Get Dressed!

It's morning... maybe you slept, maybe you didn't. Maybe you feel beautiful; maybe you don't. Maybe you have big plans today; maybe you're just hangin' with the kids. Either way,

"Girl, it's time to get Dressed!"

You've heard it said that a mom wears many 'hats.' I'm going to go a step further than that. I say we have full-blown outfits that match each hat. Oh, yeah.

And every morning, regardless of how we're feeling, we get to decide which of those outfits we're going to put on. Let's look at our options...

• We've got the **BUSY MOM.**

You know, the mom who never says "no" to anyone. She volunteers at school, and she coaches soccer. She has coffee with friends, and she sings in the choir. She babysits the neighbour's dog and serves down at the soup kitchen. She's always busy, busy, busy.

• Then there is the **ANGRY MOM.**

If your mood was a colour, would it be emo? Do you wear your irritation like a scarf around your neck? Does your make-up express itself in road-rage and gossip conversations over coffee?

• Then there's the **VICTIM MOM.**

Been there, done that. *"Nothing's working out. Kids aren't behaving. Husband isn't paying attention. I don't wanna cook. I don't wanna go out. Nobody understands. I'm all alone."* Blah blah blah. Yuck.

• Or how about the **HOME BUSINESS MOM.**

She spends all of her energy and passion on her clients. Phone calls, emails, business appointments. Kids just need to sort themselves out and not need her right now. After all, *"I'm trying to make money here. Can't you just be quiet for a while?"* Kids and husband get the leftovers, don't they?

• Or perhaps it's not money that's calling, but rather ministry… that would be the **SAINT MOM.**

She's the woman who has so much passion for God and compassion for people that she is forever giving church and ministry the number one spot in her heart and schedule. Once again, kids must just tag along and be happy to share their mom with the world.

• Then there's my personal favourite, the **MARTHA STEWART MOM** (your grandmother probably called her the "Suzie Homemaker" Mom).

You'll know if you are one because Pinterest will be your 'Bible' every day. But I get it… this one feeeeels good because the house looks amazing, and her friends compliment her on the stunning food arrangements and pillow choices on the sofa. I am totally a 'nester,' and I LOVE making my nest beautiful.

• Or perhaps you rebel at the thought of Martha Stewart and dive right into the **LAZY MOM.**

Pajamas all day, no shower, no makeup, teeth unbrushed, unwashed dishes around the house, random toys hiding the carpet… you get the picture. Now, don't get me wrong. Of course, we are all allowed to have days like this, especially when we're sick with the flu, or spending our creative energy playing with the kids. But if you're stuck in front of your phone or the TV, and this is the outfit you choose to wear every day, *"Girl, you need help."*

• Which brings me to another sensitive wardrobe choice… the **SOCIAL MEDIA MOM.** Ouch!

She's the one who is completely connected and disconnected at the same time. She has a thousand followers on Instagram, but her kids are following Netflix. She's participating in thirty cyber-conversations, but her children are aching for attention. (My friend, your phone is not going to satisfy your lonely heart when the kids finally leave the house. It's a poor substitute for REAL RELATIONSHIPS.)

Do you feel sufficiently convicted? I do. So many options. So many outfits. We can choose ANY of them… or we can choose something better.

• The **PROVERBS 31 MOM** is the best choice!

She's the woman who walks closely with God and wisely nurtures her relationship with Him. She wears kindness and love in everything she says and does. The noise and distractions that call for her attention don't move her one bit. She is attentive to the needs of her family and obeys the voice of the Father when He calls for action.

This is how the Word describes her.

> *"She is clothed with STRENGTH and DIGNITY, and she laughs without fear of the future" (Proverbs 31:25 NLT).*

> *"And above all put on LOVE, which binds everything together in perfect HARMONY" (Colossians 3:14-17 ESV).*

Here are the pieces of your Proverbs 31 Wardrobe:

- STRENGTH = the ability to resist being moved or broken by force
- DIGNITY = worthy of honour or respect
- LAUGHTER = an expression of mirth or merriment
- FEARLESS = bold, brave, and lionhearted
- LOVE = intense feelings of deep affection
- HARMONY = the simultaneous combination of sounds which bring pleasure to the hearers

YES, PLEASE! I want all of it!

BTW—just in case you are stressing about how on earth you are going to become this Proverbs 31 Mom… just relax!

Remember in the previous chapter?

You already ARE a Proverbs 31 Woman. Now walk in it.

Now, put down your phone, and go play with your kids!

LET'S CHAT...

My friends, I know that it's scary to look this honestly at ourselves. But we all have blind spots… all of us do. That's why we need each other.

♥ Of all of these wardrobe choices, be honest, which one do you wear the most often?

♥ Now ask your friend which wardrobe she sees you wear most often? (This is practical accountability. Yes, it's scary. ☺ Remember to speak truth 'in love.')

♥ What does each piece of your wardrobe practically look like when you wear it? For example: what does Strength look like? Or Dignity (which is very different than pride)? Laughter, Fearlessness, Love, Harmony?

♥ Who is going to keep you accountable for your wardrobe choices each day? Have you given someone permission to ask you the hard questions? Who?

♥ How can we practically 'change outfits' in the middle of our day?

LET'S PRAY...

Father, I am so grateful that You've given me friends who can check my blind spots... the back of my hair, the back of my shirt, and those natural behaviours that I do without thinking.

Father, I choose today to be fearless in accountability. I will not shrink back from walking in community with others, and I will courageously allow them to hold me accountable for the woman I am becoming.

I will speak love and live in harmony with my husband, my children, my family, and the people You have placed around me.

I will be strong and courageous in facing myself each day. I will run willingly to our times together, and will gladly allow You to dress me in beauty and dignity.

Today, I choose to be a PROVERBS 31 MOM!

NOTES...

NOTES...

NOTES...

4. Strip Off Everything that Slows You Down

Can we get honest here for a minute? If I were to ask you,

"What is the ONE thing that trips you up in life?"

what would you say? It's a challenging question, isn't it?

I would have to say that COMPARING MYSELF TO OTHERS is my Achilles' heel. It knocks me flat every time. Feeling confident and secure until that moment when someone else comes along… someone prettier, happier, skinnier, wealthier… more talented, more popular, more disciplined. You name it.

Do you remember in the Bible when the women were singing the praises of David in the streets, and Saul got jealous? They sang, *"Saul has slain his thousands, AND David his tens of thousands* (1 Samuel 18:7 NLT).

Did you notice the word "AND" in that verse?

David's success was never meant to be a competition between these two men. **They were mutually dependent on each other for their achievements.**

• David couldn't have done what he did without Saul making a way for him. Saul was the wise and righteous older generation who courageously led his nation into battle.

• And Saul couldn't have extended his kingdom as far without David. David was the bold and courageous younger generation who had the faith to believe God for the impossible.

Saul shouldn't have been jealous. He should have been cheering David on because this young man was the fulfillment of his leadership. **The next generation is ALWAYS meant to go higher and farther.** But instead, Saul allowed comparison and insecurity to trip him up.

My friends, comparing yourselves with those around you is NOT normal or harmless.

Comparison is an UGLY thing that we desperately need to root out of our lives. Don't tolerate it. Don't excuse it. Don't make friends with it.

I often struggle with comparing myself to others when I'm tired or feeling run down, when I let my guard down. But isn't that the nastiness of our enemy? He knows exactly when and where to strike—when we're weak, and in the point of our weakness.

If I were an athlete, I would tape up the sore muscle to keep it from further injury. If I were a soldier, I would protect my vital organs from fatal attack.

So why is it that, as Moms, we don't anticipate and protect ourselves from the dangers of Comparison? **The enemy ALWAYS attacks those he's most afraid of.**

Did you hear that?

THE ENEMY IS AFRAID OF US!

Why? Is it because we make a mean lasagna and have the cleanest toilets in town? NO! It's because we are raising the next generation, and he knows that

The next generation ALWAYS has the potential to surpass the former generation.

Psalm 112:2 (NLT) says, *"Their children will be successful everywhere; an entire generation of godly people will be blessed."*

He's talking about our kids there... yours and mine!

My friends, we need to deal ruthlessly with the spirit of comparison and strip that thing off of us, once and for all. Our kids are watching, and their destinies are at stake!

"Therefore, since we are surrounded by such a huge crowd of witnesses to the life of faith, LET US STRIP OFF EVERY WEIGHT THAT SLOWS US DOWN, especially the sin that so easily trips

us up. And let us run with endurance the race God has set before us" (Hebrews 12:1 NLT).

LET'S CHAT...

My friends, I completely understand how challenging it can be to speak about your fears and insecurities. But don't be afraid! Your freedom is just around the corner.

As we go deeper into issues of the heart, it's so important that you be fearless and get honest with each other. Confess your weaknesses out loud and bring them into the light.

Why? Because

Things hidden in darkness lose their power when they come into the light!

John 1:5 (NIV) says it this way, "The light shines in the darkness, and the darkness has not overcome it."

And Ephesians 5:8 (ESV) says, "For at one time you were darkness, but now you are light in the Lord. Walk as children of light."

And finally, John 12:46 (NIV) says, "I have come into the world as a light so that no one who believes in me should stay in darkness."

So take courage, dear friends. You can do this!

♥ Do you also struggle with comparing yourself to others? Why do you think that is?

♥ Can you recall a time when your confidence left you because someone more beautiful walked into the room (or more talented, popular, wealthy, etc.)? Tell us what happened.

♥ Do your best to name all of the things about yourself that make you feel insecure. Be brave.

♥ Have you ever been surprised to discover that someone you admire also struggles with insecurity? How did that affect you?

♥ Jealousy is usually aimed at someone in your peer group, rather than an 'enemy' outside your circle. What is the best way to stop feeling jealous of someone else? (Hint: read Matthew 5:43-48 NLT.)

"You have heard the law that says, 'Love your neighbor' and hate your enemy. But I say, love your enemies. Pray for those who persecute you! In that way, you will be acting as true children of your Father in heaven. For He gives His sunlight to both the evil and the good, and He sends rain on the just and the unjust alike.

If you love only those who love you, what reward is there for that? Even corrupt tax collectors do that much. If you are kind only to your friends, how are you different from anyone else? Even pagans do that.

But you are to be perfect, even as your Father in heaven is perfect."

♥ Even better, let's fight that jealousy in the opposite spirit. How can you encourage that person today and celebrate their strengths, rather than be intimidated by them?

Philippians 2:3-4 in The Message says, *"Don't push your way to the front; don't sweet-talk your way to the top. Put yourself aside, and help others get ahead. Don't be obsessed with getting your own advantage. Forget yourselves long enough to lend a helping hand."*

————————————♥————————————

LET'S PRAY...

Father, thank You that I have been fearfully and wonderfully made (Psalm 139:14) and You call me beautiful (Song of Solomon 4:7). You love me desperately and have called me Your masterpiece (Ephesians 2:10).

I admit that I often struggle with comparing myself to others, especially when I feel weak. Sadly, that's also when my unbelief takes over and I doubt Your love for me.

I repent for all of the times I have despised myself and called Your masterpiece worthless. I choose to be ruthless with the spirit of comparison that has tormented me for so long. I will not excuse it any longer. I will not make friends with it. I will not keep it hidden in darkness.

I choose to bless those around me who intimidate me. Help me, Father, to love them as You love them. I will not despise them because they are also Your children. I pray that You will continue to bless and prosper them as You are also blessing me.

Father of Lights, I ask You to shine the light of Your love in my heart and show me how You see me. And help me to walk as a Daughter of Light from this day on. Amen

NOTES…

NOTES...

I am a Proverbs 31
woman
blaaklistwriters.com

The image on the back is designed specifically for you!

Cut it out, frame it, or simply post it wherever you need to be inspired.

5. When the Heat Just Makes You Better

There was so much to look at. So much to observe. It was 2005, and we were having a journey of incredible firsts. First time overseas. First time in Africa *(Addis Ababa, to be exact)*. First time in a mud house. First time meeting our sponsor child.

I remember it like it was yesterday.

The sights, the smells, the sounds. The floor was pressed dirt, smooth and free from rubble. The bed was soft, the mattress old and sagging in the middle. The walls were pressed mud covered with carefully placed textiles and posters *(Jennifer Lopez appeared to be a personal favourite)* to bring colour and beauty to the atmosphere. It was cozy and clean. It was precious.

What a privilege to be so warmly welcomed into so intimate a dwelling.

Esayas's mother *(I think her name was Caroline—at least that's what it sounded like to my English ears)* puttered around, quickly and quietly, obviously nervous about her important guests.

She humbly offered us her best. The best seat, the best cup, the best plate, and I'm certain the best of her food as well. Sadly, my North American stomach struggled to accept the flavours and spices, but I managed to take two healthy bites *(one of which I swallowed twice)*.

I turned my attention to our reason for coming... Esayas, thirteen years old at the time, and his little sister. Gifts were given, smiles exchanged, and all attention centered on the contents of the backpacks. It was like Christmas in June!

I suddenly realized that smoke was filling the room. I turned to see Caroline lighting a fire inside the house. The smell of roasting coffee beans filled the air. I had NEVER smelled such aromas. It was intoxicating.

I watched with wonder and amazement as Caroline sat on the floor and stirred the beans, evenly roasting them until they had almost a burnt odor. Then she crushed them, over and over, until she was satisfied that they were fine enough; then into the stone carafe and boiling water added.

Swirling the pot in a masterful dance so that the coffee grounds remained inside, she carefully poured the coffee into her best cup for me.

I had NEVER tasted such richness in any coffee shop, ever.

It was simply the best coffee I'd ever had in my life. Not just because of the unique experience and the fantastic quality, but also because it had been made with such LOVE.

And I found myself thinking...

If my life were a cup of coffee, what quality would you taste?

Would you taste the bitter aftertaste of instant coffee, the result of poor quality beans and over-processing? Would it be bitter, or bland?

Or would you taste the richness of a life that has been through the fire?

Like the simple coffee bean, Caroline had experienced the worst life could offer her: the fire of adversity, the crushing weight of disappointment, and the scalding heat of poverty. But she hadn't allowed that to make her bitter, or worse yet, shallow and weak.

She willingly chose to sit in the mud and offer me her very best! She poured her love out on me with the best she had. Even as I'm writing this, the memory of that moment has me weeping.

What a powerful illustration of our Heavenly Father!

Philippians 2:1-11 in the SBV (Shauna Blaak Version) says, "Don't think of yourself as better than others, but rather treat others better than yourself. Be like Jesus—He WAS God, but He didn't fight for recognition as God. Instead, He emptied Himself and took the form of the lowest of servants. He humbled Himself to the lowest place of all and obeyed completely, even dying on the cross. That's why God has exalted Him HIGHER than any other power! There is nothing and no one higher than Him, and one day, EVERYONE will see and declare it!"

Jesus was the Perfect Example of Servanthood

It begs the question,

• Am I also willing to sit in the dirt and offer my very best to those who enter my personal space? My husband, kids, parents, siblings, friends, employees, etc.

• Will they enjoy the richness of my love or the bitterness of my leftovers?

I don't know if I will ever see this precious mother again on this earth. I would love to be able to hug her once more and tell her what her generous spirit has done to my heart. Perhaps, someone who knows her will one day read this and pass it on to her:

Caroline, thank you for being such an example of the Father's heart to me! I love you deeply, and I pray favour and blessing on you, your precious family, and your future and destiny!

LET'S CHAT...

In the cooking process, heat usually makes the impurities rise to the surface, right? That's one reason we heat things up before serving them.

Our hearts are often similar. The heat rises, and the gunk inside just comes bubbling to the surface, and we catch ourselves saying, *"Oops, where did that come from?"*

James 1:2 (NIV) says, *"Count it pure joy, my brothers and sisters, whenever you face trials of many kinds, because you know that the testing of your faith produces perseverance. Let perseverance finish its work so that you may be mature and complete, LACKING NOTHING."*

♥ Are you under pressure right now? Has the heat been turned up? If so, is that heat making you better or bitter?

♥ What impurities are rising to your surface? Be honest.

♥ If your life were a cup of coffee, what quality would people taste?

♥ Do those who enter your personal space (i.e., your spouse, kids, friends, co-workers, etc.) enjoy the richness of your love or the bitterness of your leftovers?

♥ Is there someone in your life who has been an excellent example of how pressure (trials and testing) has made them better? Tell us about them.

———————————♥———————————

LET'S PRAY...

Father, I really don't like stress! But I also recognize that the pressure I've been under has been causing the impurities in me to rise to the surface, and that's a good thing. Thank You for refining me.

I'm sorry, Father, when I spill that stuff on those around me instead of letting You wash it from me. I ask You to cleanse me from all of the bitterness that I've been holding in my heart toward those around me, toward my life circumstances, and sometimes even toward You. I repent for my bitterness and bad attitudes.

Father, I ask You to help me joyfully serve all of those around me. Help me to carry the aroma of Christ, and to offer my best to those who enter my personal space. Help me to smell and taste like Jesus.

Amen

———————————♥———————————

NOTES...

NOTES...

6. Do You Know How Powerful You Are?

A couple of months ago, Erwin and I took a road trip to a nearby city. And although I rarely find myself writing poetry, the weather was perfect, and I couldn't help but become a bit poetic as I gazed out of the window. Enjoy!

Dear Sky, do you realize how IMPORTANT you are?

You are the lens through which I see the sun and the stars and the world beyond.

You are the gateway for atmosphere, easily changing life as we know it down here on the ground.

When you are at peace and still, I delight in the warmth of the sun on my skin.

Images flood my mind of sun-kissed days gone by

when heat and warmth would melt away the winter blues.

Dear Sky, do you realize how VALUABLE you are?

You bring the gentle rain and water my ground, feeding tender shoots that are

just waiting for a chance to grow.

You create the clouds that give me shade

and comfort me with your breeze.

And when the weight of the world gets too much, you blow away my dust.

Dear Sky, do you realize how SCARY you are?

When you are angry, I'm afraid.

For what was meant to bless and nurture can suddenly bring fear and harm.

Like the storms that have ravaged the world beyond our borders,

your violence is frightening.

Instead of the temperate rain, the land suffers flooding, unable to absorb what you throw at it.

Too much, too quickly, 'call for help' they cry.

And instead of refreshing breezes, the wind whips and tears and destroys everything in its path.

Roofs, fences, buildings, vehicles. Order ceases, and chaos ensues.

Instead of occasional relief and shade, your angry clouds billow and roll and completely overwhelm the weak and lonely.

More than just weather, our hearts and minds suffer.

Dear Sky, why, o why, are you so angry?

Find peace and rest, and show us the sun again.

LET'S CHAT...

I don't know about you, but I've often underestimated the powerful role I have in the lives of my family.

Dear Mom, do you realize how IMPORTANT you are?

Just as the sky is the gateway for the atmosphere on the earth, **so are WE the gateways for the spiritual atmosphere in our homes.**

♥ How have you been doing in your role as gatekeeper? Have you been keeping the atmosphere in your home loving, gentle, and nurturing?

"A wise woman builds her home, but a foolish woman tears it down with her own hands" (Proverbs 14:1 NLT).

We are the gateways for the spiritual atmosphere in our homes.

♥ List some practical things you can do to make your home a more positive place to be?

Dear Mom, do you realize how SCARY you are?

Just as the sky becomes scary when it is dark and violent and blocks out the sun, **so can WE become scary** when we get angry, unpredictable, or melancholic. *"For what was meant to bless and nurture can suddenly bring fear and harm."*

To a small child, we seem very BIG, and everything we do translates bigger than we mean it to be. Our love is bigger, and our anger is bigger.

♥ Have you been guilty of letting your anger fly freely and releasing fear into the atmosphere of your home?

♥ Do you use anger and yelling as a way to manipulate your children to obey you?

Dear Mom, do you know how POWERFUL you are?

Just as the sky is the lens through which we see the sun, **so are WE the lens through which our children see the SON.**

♥ Have they been seeing Him accurately through you? Do you smell and sound like Jesus?

♥ Be specific… what are you doing well?

♥ Be specific… where can you improve?

We are the lens through which our children see the SON.

Find peace and rest, and show us the SON again.

———————————♥———————————

LET'S PRAY…

Oh, Father, there are so many times that I forget how powerful I am in the lives of my children. You have given me such a place of influence. I am not a victim.

Please forgive me for all of the opportunities that I've missed—moments when I could've shown them Your heart, but I didn't. And please forgive me also for the times when I've lost control of my temper and misrepresented Your character.

Father, I ask You to wash me clean from the failures of my past and set me free from the shame that the enemy torments me with. I am not a perfect mom, but I am not a failure either.

I am Your precious daughter, and You love me relentlessly. Thank You for empowering me now to SOUND like You, ACT like You, and SMELL like You from this moment on.

Help me to be Your hands and heart to everyone that I come in contact with. I love You and run into Your arms for comfort and strength. Amen.

NOTES...

NOTES...

NOTES...

74

I am a Proverbs 31
woman
blaaklistwriters.com

The image on the back is designed specifically for you!

Cut it out, frame it, or simply post it wherever you need to be inspired.

7. How Do You Want Them to Thank You?

I saw the most amazing commercial on TV. It was of a family sitting down for dinner, and when the mother set the food on the table, the whole family (husband and teenagers alike) screamed and CHEERED for her.

I can't even remember what the commercial was advertising, but I remember my heart leaping into my chest and thinking,

"Oh my gosh! That would be AMAZING! That's exactly what I'd like my family to do for me!"

Unrealistic? Perhaps, but it taught me something. It taught me that

I can't expect my family to meet my needs and desires until I first figure out what I WANT.

One of our pastors often says, "PEOPLE DON'T KNOW WHAT THEY DON'T KNOW." Super simple, but true. Not just in church, but in families too.

Our husbands only know what they know, and if we don't tell them what we want, how are they supposed to know?

Same goes for our kids. We can't expect them to know what we want unless we first understand it ourselves and then teach them.

So, here's my *weird twist* on mothering. In a magical world, if I could put words into my kids' mouths…

Here's How I WANT to be Thanked

Dearest Mom,

I just wanted to stop playing with my friends for a moment to tell you just how much I love and appreciate you. Thank you for everything you do for me.

Thank you for always helping me with stuff, like my homework, group projects, science projects, and other stuff that Dad isn't good at. [Haha. ok, ok, I know I'm taking my liberties here…]

Thanks for making us delicious suppers all the time. Thank you for giving up your free time to serve us. Thank you for going shopping AGAIN for glue sticks, art supplies, and more school socks. I see all of the times when you take your money and spend it on stuff we need.

We notice and we care. You are amazing, Mom!

And speaking of shopping, thanks so much for going grocery shopping ALLLLLL the time. I know we are eating everything, and it's kinda frustrating to run out of milk AGAIN, but thanks for buying more.

Thanks, Mom, for all of the times you play taxi driver for us. I know I should've told you earlier that I had another drama practice, but thank you for giving up your 'ME time' and coming anyway.

And thanks also for always being willing to take care of my friends and drive them home too. I'm proud that my friends like you, Mom.

Thanks for showing us how to learn. You are always learning something new, and it inspires me to keep learning too. I think you're the smartest Mom around and I like when you're good at stuff.

Thanks for making us play games with you. Thanks for making us read with you. Thanks for making us sit down and eat together. We have so many awesome memories just because you forced us to BE together.

Thanks for making me do my chores. I know I don't like doing them, but I'm glad that I know how to make spaghetti, clean the bathrooms, and wash and iron my clothes. I feel very powerful. Thanks for teaching me to be independent and responsible.

Thanks for loving Dad and showing us how to be a faithful wife. We know that sometimes he's grumpy, and it's hard to stay kind, but you show him kindness anyway. We can see how God helps you to love him and serve him.

And I'm proud of the way you guys flirt with each other and kiss and stuff (even though we pretend to be grossed out). I *want to be like you guys when I grow up!*

And thanks, especially, for showing us how to be faithful—not just to church but especially to God. I see when you're tired and would rather stay home, but you always keep your word. I know when you're not feeling strong, but you still do it... AND you even keep your smile on when you're tired. I love to see you singing on Sundays and leading people in worship.

Wow, Mom, I'm so proud of you!

With ♥ and kisses from your favourite child.

——————————♥——————————

LET'S CHAT...

Haha... I hope you enjoyed reading that as much as I enjoyed writing it. Yes, I want my kids to thank me like that!

Did you get the message? It's easy to identify what kind of children you want to raise, but what about you?

What kind of Mom do YOU want to be?

♥ Write an imaginary thank-you letter to yourself from your future teenager. Imagine ALL of the things you want them to notice about you, and be grateful for. *(Yes, it's ok to be silly in your letter. No, you don't have to read it to them.)*

Proverbs 31:27-29 (NLT) tells us that we can EXPECT to be praised by our kids and husbands.

"She carefully watches everything in her household and suffers nothing from laziness.

"Her children stand and bless her. Her husband praises her:

"'There are many virtuous and capable women in the world, but YOU SURPASS THEM ALL!'"

In fact, the Message Bible says it this way:

"Many women have done wonderful things, but YOU'VE OUTCLASSED THEM ALL!"

How awesome is that?!

♥ Now, use your imaginary letter to cast vision for WHO YOU WANT TO BE AS "MOM." Be specific. Be creative. Be honest.

For example:

To the best of my ability, I will feed them healthy meals.

I will willingly be a taxi-driver without giving guilt trips.

I will show kindness to my husband, even when he doesn't deserve it.

I will play with my kids and make memories whenever possible.

I will keep my word. My 'yes' will be 'yes,' and my 'no' will be 'no.'

I will not be a screaming mom.

Now, GO, and fulfill that vision!
You can do this!

LET'S PRAY...

Father, thank You that I'm not just 'shooting into the dark' here. You are giving me strategy and precision in my parenting.

I often feel overwhelmed when I think of how much I need to change. It's just too much for me. I try, and then I fail, and then I just feel like quitting. Father, I need Your strength and Your strategy to do this well.

Help me to see my POTENTIAL instead of just my weaknesses. Help me to see myself AS YOU SEE ME. Please give me fresh vision for my future and my family, and give me the strength to take little steps each day toward that goal.

Thank You that I am not a victim of my childhood, nor am I alone in this journey towards maturity. You are with me, and You've placed me in a family where I can be honest and accountable. I repent for all the times I've been too proud to let people into my personal space.

Thank You, Father, for showing me, little by little, WHO I CAN BE.

Amen.

---❤---

NOTES...

NOTES...

8. Hearing Words of Life from the Father

Let's face it... we ALL have days when our best intentions fall flat. Do you remember when I said that my Achilles' heel is comparing myself with others? Yeah, I meant it.

Comparing myself with other 'more perfect' moms knocks me flat every time. Moms who never forget their kids at school. Moms who never forget to buy milk and bread. Moms who only buy brand name clothes. Moms who look younger and prettier and skinnier than me.

You get the idea.

I recently had one-of-those-days when I felt like a complete and utter failure as a mom. Everything was going wrong, and my kids were less than pleased with my 'performance.'

So, when I got a text from my friend, it couldn't have come at a better time. She said that she'd been thinking about me and wanted to encourage me.

Her message included a recording of a prophetic word that she'd received during a season of extreme pressure with their eldest son. Her heart had been crying out, *"He is driving me crazy. I am really at the end of myself."*

The speaker on the recording didn't know anything about her—that's why his words meant so much.

She gave me permission to share this excerpt with you because she believes that it wasn't meant just for her...

GOD IS SAYING THIS TO ALL OF US.

This is what he said,

> **"I feel the Father wants to say to you that HE'S SO JOLLY PROUD OF YOU!**
>
> **He really delights in you.**
>
> **Father wants to say to you, "You're such a good Mom."**
>
> **I feel like you're facing some stuff with your children right now that you're not quite sure how to navigate, and you're just so worried about it.**
>
> **You're like, "Oh gosh, what am I going to do? How is this going to work out?"**

And Father just wants to say to you, "You're doing great. You're doing amazing."

He notices you, and He sees you exactly where you are today!

That was just what my tired soul needed to hear that day.

LET'S CHAT...

We all have strengths and weaknesses. Does the thought of throwing a kid's birthday party make you want to throw up? That's ok. Say this after me,

"Motherhood is not a performance sport."

♥ What is your button-pusher? What makes you feel like a failure?

♥ Are you feeling overwhelmed? Do you need God to speak to you today? He loves to speak to His children!

Remember, Isaiah 30:21 (NLT) says, *"Your own ears will hear him. Right behind you, a voice will say, 'This is the way you should go,' whether to the right or to the left."*

♥ Ephesians 2:10a (NLT) says, *"For we are God's masterpiece."* Wow! How does that make you feel? Do you believe it?

I am so grateful for this precious friend who radically turned my day around through her love and obedience. I needed encouragement, and God answered that prayer through human hands.

♥ Tell us about a time when you prayed for a miracle, and God answered using human hands.

♥ 2 Chronicles 16:9a (NIV) says, *"For the eyes of the LORD range throughout the earth to strengthen those whose hearts are fully committed to him."* Wow! What does that do for your heart knowing that God is looking for opportunities to encourage you?

♥ Can you think of someone in your circle who needs encouragement or support? Who is missing? Ask God how you can be the answer to her miracle today.

---❤---

LET'S PRAY...

Father, thank You for placing the lonely in families. Thank You for all of the times You've used other people to speak life to me.

Help me to humble myself, lower the walls I've built around my heart, and let people in past my pride and independence. Help me to have eyes that see Your hands, and ears that hear Your voice, even if it comes in unconventional ways.

I confess that I've listened to lies about myself for far too long. I need to hear what YOU think about me, and how YOU see me. I want to hear Your words, Father.

I worship You, God. I choose to calm the racing in my mind and allow myself to be still in Your presence.

I'm here, and I'm listening...

————————————♥————————————

NOTES...

NOTES...

I am a Proverbs 31
woman
blaaklistwriters.com

The image on the back is designed specifically for you!

Cut it out, frame it, or simply post it wherever you need to be inspired.

9. Purpose Isn't a Straight Line

If I had a dollar for every time I've heard the question *"What is God's will for my life?"* I would be a very wealthy woman.

I know you can relate. It's the question we ALL ask ourselves when we're trying to make decisions about the future, regardless of age or gender.

Now, after twenty-five years of pastoring, that question hasn't gone away. In fact, more people are asking it than ever.

Thankfully, I had a very wise person say to me years ago…

"Shauna, God's will isn't a straight line. It's more like a backyard with a lot of options and a strong fence."

What on earth does that mean? Well, let's think about it for a minute... He is a GOOD FATHER.

1. What Brings You Joy?

No good parent dictates to their children EXACTLY what they must do every minute of the day. Of course, we make sure they do their chores and help around the house; that's a regular part of family life. But that doesn't happen all day, every day.

Imagine if you will, the MOST AMAZING BACKYARD ever, full of the best toys and equipment, perfectly suited to a child's personality and tastes.

What would you see there? Perhaps a bike, skipping rope, swing set, art supplies, train set, cars and trucks, sand toys, reading books, writing books, puzzles, dolls, swimming pool. I can see it now!

How odd would it be for that child just to stand there, looking up at her father, and ask, *"What do I have to do first?"*

What do you think her daddy would say? I think he'd look at her kindly and say,

What would you LIKE to do first?

Would you like to ride your bike, and then perhaps draw some pictures? Or you could play for a while, and then we could read a book together?

Everything here is yours, my darling—YOU decide what you want to do."

My friends, that's EXACTLY what God is like with us concerning our life purpose. He loves to bless us and give us options.

How do I know that?

Because He made us in His image! And if we who are imperfect love to give our children options for fun, why would He be any different? He's not up there scheming ways to make our lives miserable. That's not in His character at all.

He is a loving Father, and He created you IN HIS STYLE.

Recognizing what brings you joy is a good place to start when trying to discover your life purpose. In fact, those dreams that are lying deep inside of you... HE PLACED THEM THERE TO BEGIN WITH.

Get to know Your Father, and let Him develop and mature those dreams.

2. Your Boundaries Have Fallen in Pleasant Places

The next thing to consider are the boundaries that He's given you. No, I'm not going to debate about what's fair and what's not. Boundaries are a good thing—get over it.

THE FENCE TEST: Some years ago, I remember hearing of a university group that studied the effects that FENCES had on elementary-school children (Kindergarten to Grade 6).

Do you know that, in the schools WITHOUT fences, the children subconsciously played closer to the school building and didn't even get close to the outer limits of the playground? I seem to recall that they only used about 35% of the playground, probably because they felt safer closer to the buildings.

But in the schools that HAD a fence, those children played everywhere and anywhere. They displayed more confidence and boldness, and they even played right up against the fence line.

They used ALL of the space allowed and MAXIMIZED THEIR FUN!

How cool is that?

My friends, that's what God has done for us. He has given us strong boundaries to protect us from decisions and influences that would otherwise hurt us.

Psalm 16:6 (NIV) says it this way, *"The boundary lines have fallen for me in pleasant places; surely I have a delightful inheritance."*

Proper boundaries will ALWAYS make you feel more confident and more alive.

Healthy boundaries maximize our fun!

How can you discover what your purpose is?

1. **Read the Bible.** There, you'll find both His promises and His boundaries for you. He will never ask you to do something contrary to what He's said in His Word.

2. **Pray and listen.** God loves to speak to His children.

   Isaiah 30:21 (NLT) says, *"Your own ears will hear him. Right behind you, a voice will say, 'This is the way you should go,' whether to the right or to the left."*

3. **Walk with pastors/teachers/mentors** who can help you grow in maturity. Christianity is not a drive-through. It takes time to mature, but it's always worth the effort.

And the next time you want to complain and say, *"God, I'm bored. What should I do now?"* just remember

---

Fun is your responsibility.

And then decide what you'd like to do first.

———————————♥———————————

LET'S CHAT...

My friends, please don't feel bad for not knowing the answers to these questions immediately. You've focused on everyone else for a long time, and it's normal to lose yourself in the chaos.

So, relax... take some time... and search your heart.

It's time to REDEFINE your IDENTITY and purpose as a woman.

♥ In one minute or less, tell us what your Life Purpose is. (Define what you already know.) Maybe start with,

"I am on this earth to..."

"My purpose in life is to..."

"My reason for living is to..."

♥ Ask yourself these questions often and regularly, especially when you hit a new season in life.

What am I good at? (Don't say "nothing." We are all good at something.) Make a list of all of your talents, skills, and giftings.

What am I passionate about? What do I love to do? What gives me energy and joy?

♥ What are healthy boundaries? Have a conversation with the group and consider ALL of the different aspects of boundaries: moral, physical, mental, psychological, emotional, relational, spiritual.

♥ Are there boundaries that you've been crossing? If so, repent quickly. Then ask someone you trust to hold you accountable in that area.

Remember: boundaries are not your enemy. Don't fight them. They are there to protect you, give you safety and security, and maximize your fun.

♥ Welcome the Father into your process of defining your IDENTITY. Ask Him to help you put your Life's Purpose into words. He's more excited than anyone about the plans He has for your life!

"For I know the plans I have for you," says the Lord. "They are plans for good and not for disaster, to give you a future and a hope" (Jeremiah 29:11 NLT).

LET'S PRAY...

Thank You, Father, that You have better plans for my life than I can even hope or imagine.

I realize that I've been so busy that I've starved my spirit, neglected my soul, and lost myself to kid chaos. In some areas, I don't even know what I like to do anymore. Please help me to bring order to every part of me.

I repent for all of the times I've crossed the boundaries You've given me, whether it be in my actions, or words, or even just in my thoughts. I ask You to wash me clean and cover me with Your grace. Fill me with Holy Spirit so I can live like the new creation I am.

I invite You to speak to me and help me define my Life's Purpose. Yesterday is gone, and tomorrow isn't here yet. I welcome You to redefine my identity today.

Father, I am so grateful that You know everything about me, and You've prepared a life that is perfect for ME. I choose again to trust You with my life, my family, and my future.

You are a good, good Father.

Amen

NOTES...

NOTES...

NOTES...

10. No More Lies—It's Time for the Truth

I'd never heard John 4:24 like I heard it that night, laying face down on the worn carpet and deeply overcome by God's presence. Carpet time. Surrounded by friends who had grown far closer to me than just fellow choir members; these were my people. I knew them. I trusted them. I loved them.

It was our annual worship team retreat—a time for the worshippers on the frontline to recharge themselves, reconnect with each other, and renew their passion for God.

"For God is Spirit, so those who worship Him must worship in spirit and IN TRUTH."

Have you ever noticed the word "truth" in that verse? Worshiping in truth… what does that even mean?

The speaker asked the question, *"Has the enemy been labelling you with names that don't belong to you? Has he been speaking words of death over you when you're feeling weak or alone?"*

It was time to get honest with ourselves and identify the lies we'd been believing—word curses that the enemy would whisper in the middle of the night, like: *"You're such a failure. You've always been a loser. You're insignificant. Invisible. Liability. Burden."*

Ohhh… *those* labels.

It was a powerful time of getting real with ourselves and with each other. Tears flowed freely as precious sons and daughters of the Most High acknowledged the word curses that had held them captive for so long.

How incredibly liberating to admit those things out loud. Out of the darkness and into the light.

But we weren't stopping there. Now that the lie was exposed, the leader challenged us to ask God for the TRUTH.

> **"Father, with all my heart I want to worship You in both spirit and in truth. Who do YOU say that I am? By what name do YOU call me?"**

I remember laying face down on the carpet as I let the tears running freely from eyes to cheeks to floor.

Time seemed to stand still, but one by one, you could hear people getting breakthrough. It wasn't long until the room was ringing with the sounds of joy and laughter.

Old labels were being removed, new names issued, and new identities embraced.

- No longer 'Failure' but 'Joy.'
- No longer 'Insignificant' but 'Conqueror.'
- No longer 'Loser' but 'Beloved.'

That night was a turning point for our worship team. Like Sarah who went from being Sarai (quarrelsome) to Sarah (princess), we went from being great to faaaantastic. (Genesis 17:15)

We had always been a great team before, but **after having an encounter with Almighty God and coming away with new names and new identities, we walked in brand new confidence and anointing.**

That's what TRUTH does.
It unlocks destiny!

Getting on stage and leading worship after that weekend was so different. We were fearless, bold. We had finally seen ourselves AS GOD SAW US and it changed how we led.

My friends, you can't reach your fullest potential if you are living according to the lies spoken by the enemy.

That's what John 4:24 means.

"... those who worship Him must worship in spirit and IN TRUTH."

What was my new name?

For years, I had struggled with insecurity, never wanting to bother people when I needed help. I would rather burn myself out than be an inconvenience. That night, God told me that I was no longer 'Inconvenient,' but He called me 'Mother.'

To be honest, I didn't really understand what was so special about God calling me 'Mother.' I mean, I already had a bunch of kids, so it was kind of anti-climactic. I was hoping for a cooler name like 'awesome' or 'powerful' or 'diva.'

"God, why 'Mother?' That's kind of boring."

His answer was simply, *"Trust Me. I know what I'm doing."*

More than fifteen years have passed since that night, and I've seen God grow this calling on my life to be 'mom' to those around me. Moms at school, moms at church, moms of babies, moms of teens. He wasn't just telling me that I was a mother, He was calling and anointing me to BE a mother.

It's so exciting! I've got an incredible love for moms, no matter what their age or situation, and I've felt Him fill me with HIS love for each of them. What a privilege to see His Word fulfilled in my life!

———————————————♥———————————————

LET'S CHAT...

I think it's safe to say that ALL OF US, at one time or another, have believed the enemy's lies over us. He's a rotten liar, but he manages to make us believe that his lies are true.

The one thing we discovered personally during that retreat was this:

Things hidden in darkness lose their power when they come into the light!

♥ When the lights are out and your emotions depleted, do you hear the enemy speaking words of death over you? What are they? *(Don't be afraid to say them out loud. Get them out of the darkness and into the light.)*

♥ What does the Bible say about those lies?

♥ Here are some Scriptures that speak about our true Identity. Read them. Memorize them. Write them on post-it notes and stick them around the house. Do whatever you have to do to speak truth to yourself.

2 Corinthians 5:17 – You are a new creation.

Ephesians 4:24 – You are righteous and holy.

2 Corinthians 5:18 – You are reconciled to God.

John 15:16 – You are chosen by God.

Song of Solomon 4:7 – You are altogether beautiful.

Psalm 139:14 – You are fearfully and wonderfully made.

Matthew 5:14 – You are the light of the world

1 Thessalonians 5:5 – You are children of the light.

Matthew 5:13 – You are the salt of the earth.

2 Corinthians 4:6 – You are a carrier of His divine light.

Romans 8:37 – You are more than a winner.

Hebrews 3:1 – You have a heavenly calling.

I Peter 2:9 – You are royalty.

Ephesians 2:10 – You are God's masterpiece.

Romans 8:17 – You are co-heirs with Christ.

Ephesians 4:14-15 – You are mature and stable.

Zechariah 8:16 – You are called to speak Truth.

Ephesians 1:4 – You were chosen before creation.

Ecclesiastes 3:11 – He has made you beautiful.

Jeremiah 29:11 – You have a great future.

♥ Get alone with God. He WANTS to speak new life to you more than you even want to receive it. Don't be in a rush. Worship, pray, and wait. I know it may feel impossible with kids running around and crazy 'mom-responsibilities.'

"Father, we're asking for a miracle. Orchestrate the children today to play, sleep, or do whatever for as long as You need them to, and help these beautiful mommies escape for a much-needed encounter with You!"

The Message Bible says it this way in Matthew 6:6,

"Here's what I want you to do: Find a quiet, secluded place so you won't be tempted to role-play before God. JUST BE THERE AS SIMPLY AND HONESTLY AS YOU CAN MANAGE. The focus will shift from you to God, and you will begin to sense His grace."

♥ Ask the Father, **"Who do YOU say that I am?**

By what name do YOU call me?

What is my true identity?"

LET'S PRAY...

Father, thank You for loving me so intensely and for having better plans for my life than I can even imagine. I choose to trust You again with my family, my finances, and my future.

I confess that I've believed the lies of the enemy for far too long. He's been calling me all sorts of names, and I've believed him. Names like _____________ (fill in the blank here).

Father, I desperately want to be free from the self-hatred and shame that I've been living under. Please tune my ears to hear Your still small voice.

Speak to me, Lord. I'm listening.

———————————❤———————————

NOTES...

NOTES...

NOTES...

blaaklistwriters.com
She laughs without fear of the future
blaaklistwriters.com

The image on the back is designed specifically for you!

Cut it out, frame it, or simply post it wherever you need to be inspired.

11. Manifesto of Motherhood

They say that "Hindsight is 20/20" and I couldn't agree more. Looking back now, I've had such a wealth of love and experience in my journey as "Mom."

*   Was I the perfect mom? Not a chance.

*   Do I deserve a first place trophy for MomAwesomeness? *(Oooh, wouldn't that be nice?)* No, I'm afraid there will always be someone more awesome.

*   Was I real? Definitely.

*   Did I do my best with what I knew at the time? Absolutely!

If only I could relive those early years with the wealth of **knowledge, wisdom, and the healthy dose of 'perspective'** that I now possess.

I'm not ready for teenagers to leave home and head to college! I've finally mastered the art of raising toddlers, managing homework, and wading through the hormonal years.

So, my dear friends, if I were to turn back the clock and start the MOM-journey again,

This is what I would say...

This is what I would promise...

This is what I believe about parenting...

———————————❤———————————

MY MANIFESTO OF MOTHERHOOD

[We took this pic just before moving from Canada to South Africa]

❤ I WILL LOVE YOU, each one of you, uniquely and passionately! I will not show favourites. There will never be a competition for who has more of my heart, for with every child that is added to this family, just like *The Grinch who Stole*

Christmas, my heart will "grow three sizes in one day." I will not run out of love for you.

♥ I will love you by FEEDING MY SOUL with good things so that I have an overflow of love and acceptance to give you. I will take 'ME-time' regularly and not let myself become depleted. I will feed my mind with things that stimulate, educate, and inspire. I will always learn something new so that you can follow my footsteps.

♥ I will love you by LOVING MY BODY that nurtures you. Not just for nine months, I'm talking about forever. To the best of my ability, I will stay strong and healthy. Like Proverbs 31:17 (NKJV) says, *"She girds herself with strength, and strengthens her arms."*

♥ I will love you by FEEDING MY SPIRIT with God, the true and living God. It is He who empowers me to speak and behave like His heart toward you. I will read the Word, I will pray, and I will worship so that the atmosphere in our home feels as familiar to you as the place you just came from.

♥ I will SERVE YOU FAITHFULLY, even when you wake me up… again. I will prepare for those long nights when you suffer 'baby jetlag' and decide to play rather than sleep. Perhaps we will sing, perhaps we will cuddle, or perhaps I will read books that take me on my own adventure so that we can enjoy the night hours together.

♥ I will patiently teach you to ORGANIZE your toys and clean up your mess before starting another so that we can live in order and enjoy it. It's never too early to be an *Organization Diva'* (sorry, boys, *'Organization Master'*).

♥ I will MAKE A MESS with you more often. It's creative, it's stimulating, and it's downright fun!

♥ I will give you permission to HATE certain foods, but I'll also teach you to keep trying them because you never know when your taste buds might change. *"Today might be the day!"*

♥ I will love and EMBRACE YOU whenever you need me, but I will also gently and patiently teach you to SLEEP in your own bed. Yes, it may take hours of camping on your floor and holding your hand through the bars, but you'll grow in confidence and peace of mind. You are worth it.

♥ I will regularly sneak into your room while you're sleeping and KISS YOU GOODNIGHT. Don't fight it—it's just what Moms do. Someday, you'll miss that.

♥ I will PLAY on the floor with you as much as possible. Puzzles, trains, cars, Barbies, or whenever you just need some attention. You name it, let's play. Dishes can wait.

♥ I will READ TO YOU, regularly and faithfully. I will stop the busyness of my evening schedule, put the chores on hold, and ignore the emails a while longer, just so that we can explore Narnia together. (Those memories with you still keep me warm on rainy days.)

♥ I will teach you MUSIC, art, and creativity! Paying customers will have to stand-in-line because you are worth the investment.

♥ I will teach you that, even though school may not be fun right now, you can ENJOY THE FEELING OF KNOWLEDGE. It feels good to know stuff. Learning is FUN! Everyone learns—even Mommy and Daddy learn.

♥ I will not protect you from boredom. FUN IS YOUR RESPONSIBILITY. In fact, boredom is a critical ingredient for creativity and discovery. *"Go, make some fun."*

♥ I will teach you to BE KIND by how I speak to you, how I discipline you, how I serve you, and how I treat your dad. From my mouth and my actions, you will regularly hear the words, *"Stay sweet."*

♥ I will help you FACE YOUR FEARS by showing you when I face mine. Spiders, snakes, sharks, and yes, even birds. You will see me conquer my fears, moment-by-moment, day-by-day, so that you can also conquer yours.

♥ I will stop, listen, and HEAR YOU when you speak to me. I will also teach you to be respectful and patient while you wait for your turn to speak (after all, there are usually five people needing my attention at the same time).

♥ I will CELEBRATE YOUR LIFE with honour and significant celebration each time you have a birthday or special event. Parties celebrate the miracle of another year together!

♥ I will teach you to BE GENEROUS with your time, your efforts, your love, and your possessions. I know it may feel like you can't make everyone happy, but that's ok. Like Mother Theresa said, *"Give your best anyway."*

♥ I will teach you to BE POWERFUL—laundry, cooking, cleaning, yard work. Knowing stuff is empowering. And I will also teach you to SERVE WELL as you learn these things. Family chores are normal and healthy. You don't get paid for serving—chores are your rent for living in our house and eating our food. You belong.

♥ I will show you that you CAN do things you don't like to do, and it won't kill you. Dad and I do it all the time. It's ok. "YOU'RE WELCOME TO HATE IT, BUT YOU STILL HAVE TO DO IT."

Too many people shortchange their success in life because they never learned to push past their 'feelings.'

♥ I will INVEST in your gifts and talents. You are worth extra math tutoring, guitar lessons, drum lessons, voice lessons, and chemical peels at the skin clinic. You are worth it!

♥ I will create memories and FAMILY TRADITIONS and show you how to make a 'HOME' wherever you are. I will show you how to be 'Family.'

♥ I will INVITE PEOPLE into our home and, in so doing, will show you how to honour those who are different from you. The world is so big. (By the way, this is also the best way to deal with homesickness—**loneliness is best cured by opening up your heart to others.)**

♥ I will open up our home for your FRIENDS, and I will teach you to recognize which friends are good for you and which ones are not. But I will also allow you to make bad choices without an "*I told you so*" at the end. There will always be an open door here.

♥ I will stay awake and PRAY like crazy until the key turns in the door and I know that you are home safe and sound. That's just what Moms do.

♥ I will show you that weak people also WORSHIP. Yes, I may be grumpy on the way to church, but that won't stop me from completely engaging God in worship. No, it doesn't make me a hypocrite. In fact, worshipping fully makes me a better mom because it washes out the 'grumpy me' and fills me with Jesus.

♥ I will show you how to love and honour your future spouse by HOW I TREAT YOUR DAD, even when he doesn't deserve it (and vice versa). We will model forgiveness and real love in front of you.

♥ I will show you Jesus by BEING REAL ABOUT MY FAITH and allowing you to participate in my process. We will pray together for a miracle, and then rejoice together at the breakthrough. We will talk openly about spiritual things and allow you to discover Jesus for yourself.

♥ I will willingly ALLOW MY HEART TO BREAK when my little birdies leave the nest. And even though it may take you thousands of miles away, I will be happy for you because I will know that you are doing exactly what God has set before you. And despite the fact that food will cease to have flavour for three months, I will choose to RELEASE YOU TO YOUR DESTINY.

♥ And once you are no longer under my roof, I WILL PRAY EVEN MORE for you, knowing that our Father has your life in His hands, and

---

He wants the best for you even more than I do!

His plans for you are good! Your destinies are sure!

———————♥———————

LET'S CHAT...

My friends, I shared my manifesto with you, not to make you feel overwhelmed or intimidated, but to inspire you to

dream bigger and aim higher!

You have the incredible privilege to be your kid's Mom, whether they are five years old or 55 years old. God didn't give you that responsibility lightly, and He doesn't make mistakes.

You are the PERFECT person to be their Mom!

How do I know that?

> Because Ecclesiastes 3:11 (NLT) says, *"God has made everything beautiful for its own time. He has planted eternity in the human heart, but even so, people cannot see the whole scope of God's work from beginning to end."*

Just because you can't see His full plan for your life yet, doesn't mean that you aren't in the right place at the right time.

Rest in it. Embrace it. Own it.

Will you ever reach a state of perfection in your motherhood? No, but that isn't the goal anyway. The goal of our lives is to walk closely with Holy Spirit, to love Jesus with all of our hearts, and be an accurate reflection of our Heavenly Father.

To be able to say at the end of our lives,

"I did the best I could with what I knew, and God made up the difference."

How beautiful is that?!

But, perhaps your kids are grown already, and you're feeling waves of regret right now. It's not too late, my friend. As long as there is breath in your lungs, **you can STILL be the Proverbs 31 Woman.**

Your Father STILL has incredible plans for your life!

His 'Blank Cheque' is STILL yours for the taking. God has written your name there and signed it with His blood. Don't just believe Him for pennies when He has immeasurable wealth for you.

Haggai 2:9 (NLT), says, *"THE FUTURE GLORY OF THIS TEMPLE WILL BE GREATER than its past glory, says the Lord of Heaven's Armies. And in this place, I will bring PEACE. I, the Lord of Heaven's Armies, have spoken!"*

You are that Temple and the future looks awesome! It doesn't matter what happened in the past.

Isaiah 43:18 (NLT) says, *"But forget all that—it is nothing compared to what I am going to do."*

So, shake off the regret. Cast off the shame.

This is not about perfection—it's about walking closely with the Father and letting His presence and power fill you each day.

I don't want to live with regret.

I don't want to say, *"I wish I could do it all again."*

At the end of my life, I want to laugh with delight and shout out loud,

"Yay, God! We won!"

My friends, I have one last assignment for you...

♥ Write out your own Manifesto of Motherhood using your children's names. Declare the truth about who God says YOU are, and who God says THEY are. Let this manifesto set the tone for your home and the flavour for your family.

And one day, be prepared to pass it on to them when they become parents themselves. It can be a powerful tool to speak purpose and identity to them too.

And always remember,

You ARE a Proverbs 31 Woman AND your Heavenly Father loves you very much.

———————————————♥———————————————

LET'S PRAY...

Father, what a privilege it has been to take this journey together. Thank You for setting me free from lies. Thank You for speaking truth and destiny to the deepest parts of me. Thank You for empowering me to keep going and not quit.

I repent for all of the times I've 'lived in the past,' rehearsing the old things and remembering the old hurts.

I choose today to forget those former things, and to fix my eyes on You alone. I choose to shake off EVERYTHING that weighs me down... shame, guilt, regret, comparison... and to believe You for the BEST for my life.

I declare that You are a Good Father, and You have good plans for my life and the lives of my family.

I choose to believe Your Word for me.

I love you God more than anything else around me. I worship You and I commit my ways to you again.

I choose to look forward and not backward, to press on and not shrink back, and to laugh without fear of the future.

I am Your beautiful girl, and I always will be. Amen.

NOTES...

NOTES...

I am a Proverbs 31
woman
blaaklistwriters.com

The image on the back is designed specifically for you!

Cut it out, frame it, or simply post it wherever you need to be inspired.

About Shauna

Shauna is happily married to her college sweetheart, Erwin, and together they have four amazing children who have grown up as PKs, MKs, and TCKs *(Pastor's kids, Missionary kids, and Third Culture Kids)*. For the last decade, they've been living in South Africa and pastoring the worship ministry at Victory Church in Jeffreys Bay.

She knows better than most the challenges that come with being the *SuperMom of an International Family*. Together, they've weathered the toddler years, the school years, the teenage years, culture shock, homesickness, and the drama of living overseas.

With one child now living in Australia, another in Canada, and the youngest two still in South Africa with them, Shauna has a wealth of wisdom to share with other moms who are perhaps asking themselves, *"Who the heck am I?"*

Her life message is simply this...

You ARE a Proverbs 31 Woman, and you were never meant to walk alone!

You can find her blogging at www.blaaklistwriters.com

Contact

To contact Shauna or book her for your next Women's Event, you can reach her at:

Email: shauna.blaak@gmail.com
Website: www.blaaklistwriters.com

In South Africa:
P.O. Box 3232
9 De Reyger St
Jeffreys Bay, Eastern Cape
South Africa 6330
Phone: +27 83 375 3518

In Canada:
6408 14 Avenue NW
Edmonton, Alberta
Canada T6L 1S4
Phone: +1 780 463 2401

SOCIAL MEDIA
Facebook: www.facebook.com/shauna.blaak
                www.facebook.com/blaaklistwriters
Instagram: @shaunablaak
Twitter: @blaaklistwriter
YouTube: www.youtube.com/channel/UCpa_ViTS57VIlPZ43za1Qkg

Coming Soon

If you loved this book, you're also gonna love

Book #2 in the MomAwesomeness Series!

www.ingramcontent.com/pod-product-compliance
Lightning Source LLC
Chambersburg PA
CBHW060941050726
47592CB00003B/1050